NEARLY A CARESS.

PURE
LEAF
BREWED TEA

NEARLY A CARESS

Last Poems by

JANE GREER

Critical Introduction by
ROBERT BERNARD
HASS

PITTSBURGH:
Lambing Press
2026

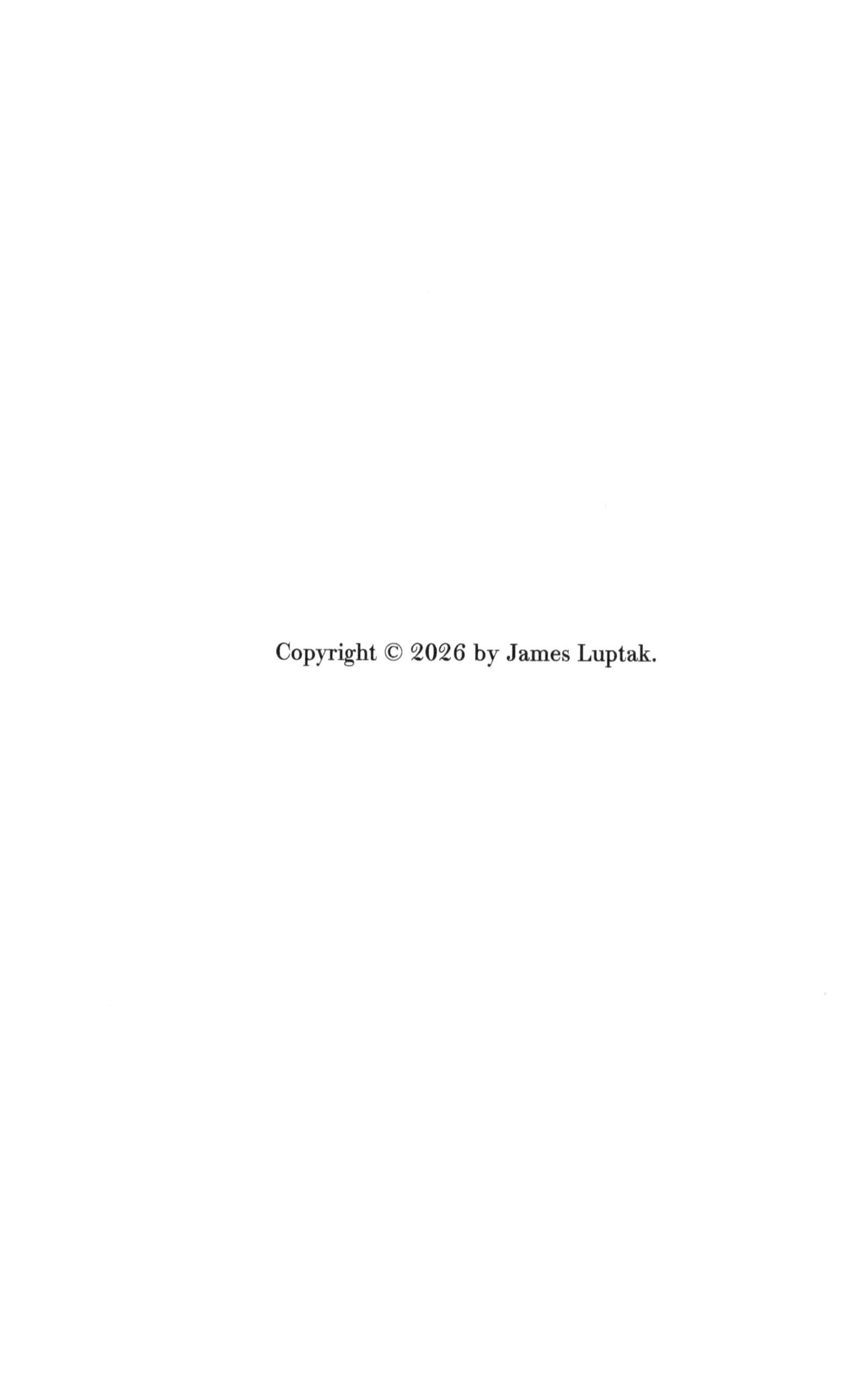

CONTENTS

Plains Jane: A Critical Introduction
  by Robert Bernard Hass   ix

Packed Carefully Away   1

In the Activities Room   2

Nothing is Needful Here   3

That by Which We Rise   4

Long Covid   5

Quarantine   6

Shallow   7

Eiswein   8

So Great Was My Want   9

Almost As If   10

Here in the Stadium   11

In None of Her Other Ages   12

We'd Like Them to Be Different Than They Are   13

What Sort of Light   14

His Teeth on Your Synapses   15

Prayer for Sister Claire   16

Second Summer   17

Fragment   18

The Last Kind Thing   19

The Triolet is Such a Bore   20

Minus Ninety-seven   21

About the Poet   23

PLAINS JANE

A Critical Introduction by
Robert Bernard Hass

When I remember the poet Jane Greer, it's not
the scrupulous journal editor staunchly defend-
ing traditional forms that I see. Nor do I see the
fiercely independent woman staring beyond
her window at the hogbacks and badlands
bathed in the expansive winter light of her
beloved North Dakota. The person I see in-
stead is the marvelously talented poet I had the
great fortune to meet later in her life. As I
imagine her even now, I see her sitting at her
desk and wrestling with poems that reconcile
herself to her mortality. I hear the voice of our
many conversations, either in person or online,
her distinct patois that of a deeply introspective
and witty poet slowly awakening, as she writes
in "In None of Her Other Ages," "from what

had seemed a dream" to realize that "[t]hings are ending, or have ended, or will end." At the close of this poem she asserts that, despite the natural deterioration of the body, "There is no nothingness." She is careful not to divulge with certainty what the absence of "nothingness" might be; nevertheless, her quiet and enduring confidence that "something" exists beyond the grave provides her, and us, with a measure of consolation.

Nearly a Caress is indeed a book of reckonings, composed by one contemplating the joy, beauty and confusion of her declining years. Its poems do not announce themselves with rupture, regret, or confession. Instead, they proceed by formal compression and paradox. Her language is filled with expressive beauty, but what must be privately borne remains unspoken. Across these dignified poems—verses shaped by illness, quarantine, devotion, loss, and a fierce attentiveness to the natural world—Jane develops a poetics of restraint in which suffering is neither denied nor theatrically displayed. Pain circulates, returns, and refigures itself, but she characteristically constrains it within tightly constructed forms that both acknowledge damage and refuse despair.

The title of this posthumous collection, drawn from "Packed Carefully Away," reveals the book's governing tension: Loss exacts a cost that "now seems nearly a caress," an astonishing idea in which injury is neither erased nor denied, but rendered intimate, tactile, and miraculously tender. The poem insists on secrecy—"all kept in secret, forming no part of speech"—even as it speaks. Throughout this book, Jane's work repeatedly occupies the liminal threshold between articulation and silence, between exposure and preservation. What the tide can smooth, it will; what it cannot reach must be carefully packed away. This is not repression but reverence, a recognition that our most precious truths are sometimes altered by utterance and therefore must remain ineffable.

Jane's characteristic formal poise reinforces this ethic. Many of these poems are short, tightly wrought, and metrically regular, often drawing on hymn, epigram, or devotional lyric. Rhyme and stanza act not as ornament but as discipline, a way of keeping faith with experience without allowing it to sprawl into unearned sentimentality or dejection. Jane's brilliant, compressed technique is clearly on display in "That by Which We Rise." In a poem reminiscent of Frost or Dickinson's finest brief lyrics, paradox becomes both subject and structure: the poem turns insistently on itself, a theological axiom rendered with a childlike clarity that is anything but simple. Salvation here is not sentimental; it is procedural—"salvation's protocol"—and its "mean and small" logic is as severe as it is consoling.

The deeply Catholic religious imagination that informs *Nearly a Caress* is neither doctrinaire nor abstract. Jane's poems are sacramental in the best sense of the word, as she locates in tangible language the holiness embedded in material things and human actions. In "In the Activities Room," a hibiscus flower becomes both "sacrament and synecdoche," its ephemeral blaze mirroring "holy brevity / which, in a day, is evermore." This doubleness—transience as eternity—is one of Jane's most frequently recurring themes. Similarly, "Eiswein" finds sweetness intensified by deprivation, a wine "fancied for what she lost," its warmth "burned clean away / in that cold holocaust." The language in this poem is exacting, unflinching, and ethically alert. The poem refuses to aestheticize suffering even as it traces how loss can concentrate meaning. Contrasting these examples, the light-hearted and charming "So Great was My Want" stages a delicate drama of desire and patience as the speaker courts a wild crow. The crow's final gift—a key to some "sturdy box"—suggests that our comprehension of the most important divine gifts will take time. The deepest meaning arrives obliquely, as grace often does, and can only be fully understood when we awaken from this dream of life and enter another realm of being.

While many of the poems in Nearly a Caress offer us personal meditations, Jane is careful to situate personal suffering within our collective historical moments—pandemic, quarantine, and illness—and by doing so reinforces the idea that shared suffering is the origin of compassion. "Quarantine," for example, frames isolation as potential spiritual renewal. With the proper "wit" and mindset one can transform the imperfect days of "suffering and resurrection" into "praise." In "Long Covid," Jane maps pain's migratory propensities onto the body's remembered injuries. The poem's final line—"Long covid is a lot like love"—does not trivialize affliction. Instead, it acknowledges love's capacity to reawaken old vulnerabilities, to arrive without warning, to lodge itself painfully where history once awakened love's promise for a meaningful life.

As a posthumous collection, *Nearly a Caress* invites us to read these poems not as final statements but as meditations upon an ongoing moral, aesthetic, and spiritual journey. What Jane leaves us is not closure but example, a way of attending to the world that honors damage without surrendering to it, that finds joy in suffering, that knows when to speak and when to pack something carefully away.

In a letter to a dear friend just weeks before her passing, Jane wrote, "The best things in life are small, quiet, and cheap. I am learning to subtract more than I add... Isn't that how a poem gets perfected? Maybe I am becoming my own poem." As Jane's work evolved into the poems that comprise this book, her journey toward perfection by diminishment ironically enlarges her accomplishment. If the end of human action is virtue, and the end of human reason truth, Jane's last poems reflect an ongoing aesthetic journey toward goals she acknowledges she can never fully attain in this

life. The humble wisdom inherent in these poems reminds us that, even as we age, the journey toward these teleological goals persists,
even if the answers to the great mysteries of
our lives remain elusive, to be satisfied only by
our long-awaited beatific vision.

PACKED CAREFULLY AWAY

It seemed an endless season of letting go,
and what was lost, surrendered, none will guess.
The tide will always smooth the battered beach
and the charred heart of the wood burst forth in
    green.

And all that was given up no one will know,
nor the cost which now seems nearly a caress:
all kept in secret, forming no part of speech.
Embers will cool and sands be made pristine.

All kept in secret, saved but pressed down low,
packed carefully away with a muttered blessing.
Tide cannot alter what it cannot reach.
The charred heart of the wood remains unseen.

IN THE ACTIVITIES ROOM

No one will say it, but we know
today's fresh-flamed hibiscus flower
reveals in one brief, glorious show
our birth, our life, our final hour.

Sacrament and synecdoche
live in a pot near the atrium door,
mirroring holy brevity
which, in a day, is evermore.

NOTHING IS NEEDFUL
HERE

Whatever I might have wanted,
I didn't expect a thing.
Be easy. Breathe slowly.
Nothing is needful here.
See: I take three steps back
and turn my face away
that I might be allowed to stay.

THAT BY WHICH WE RISE

That by which we rise
is that by which we fall.
This comes as no surprise at all.
But paradox the rule,
that by which we fall
is also that by which we rise.
This may seem cruel—
this may seem mean and small
of God—but there it lies:
salvation's protocol.

LONG COVID

It moves around, my friend reports,
to where her body suffered hurts
at various moments in her past.
Here, where she crashed her bike at nine
and cracked a rib, it hurts again,
although it shows up on no test;
now in her healed meniscus, now
in her lower back, old pain is new,
old random injuries revive.
On rising, she cannot foresee
which part of her will hurt that day.
Long covid is a lot like love.

QUARANTINE

In this extraordinary time
we sit and sigh and wait for it
to end, but if we had the wit
to recognize the paradigm
of suffering and resurrection
we would be on our knees in praise
that we were given all these days,
so perfect in their imperfection.

SHALLOW

I shake my head at myself in rueful disbelief:
what I had thought my theme is merely a motif
that comes and goes. I shake my head at myself
    and sigh
because for the crime of fraud I have no alibi.
I shake my head at the thin and friable veneer
I wear to hide my essence threatening to appear.
So shallow, and so sorry that this is what I bring,
I shake my head and make my same old offering.

EISWEIN

She was left long on the vine,
unpicked till the first hard frost.
Now she is sweet and intense,
and fancied for what she lost:
some warmth, burned clean away
in that cold holocaust.

SO GREAT WAS MY WANT

I dreamed I made friends with a wild crow.
I sat very still and did not twitch
when he landed near me, and we eyed each
    other
for a long moment, both of us still,
wary but ready for a pleasant surprise,
and then he took himself away.
The same thing happened three days in a row.
On the fourth, I laid a thick slice of orange
On the grass just out of my arm's reach,
And he walked around it, looking at it
But really looking at me, and I sat
Looking at him and did not twitch,
Not a muscle, not a hair, so great was my want.
Then he grabbed it and took himself away.
The next day, there in the grass, was a key,
A shiny key, to some sturdy box,
Which I would need to wake to discover.

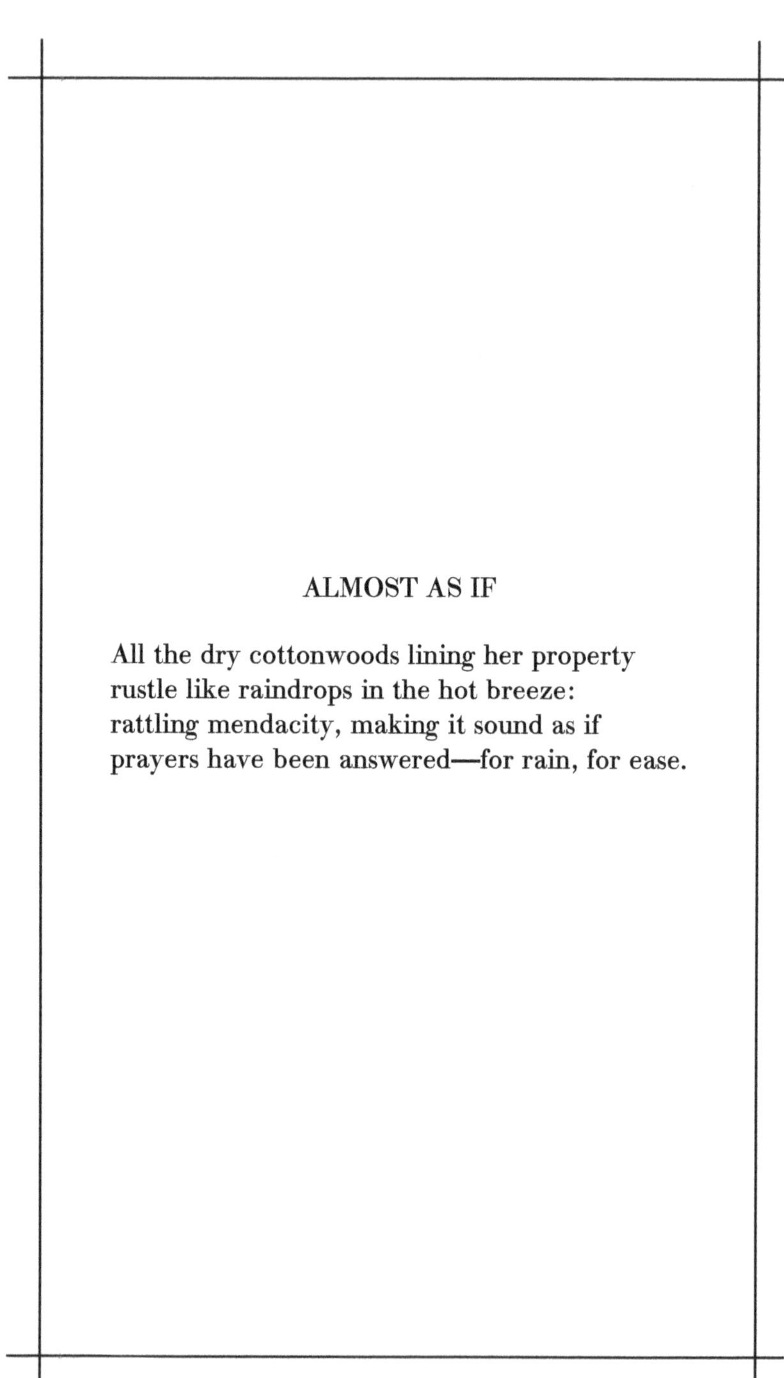

ALMOST AS IF

All the dry cottonwoods lining her property
rustle like raindrops in the hot breeze:
rattling mendacity, making it sound as if
prayers have been answered—for rain, for ease.

HERE IN THE STADIUM

Here in the stadium,
what is this fragrance
damping our revelry?
Bread baking. Incense.

Oh, it's just Polycarp
on his bright pyre—
stubborn old Polycarp
not on fire.

No need to nail me,
he'd said—my Lord
will help me stay tethered
by your thin cord.

Hands bound behind him—
unblemished ram—
he stands in the holocaust
singing some hymn.

The world is off-kilter,
our afternoon ruined
by incense and baking bread
and no one burned.

IN NONE OF HER OTHER AGES

In none of her other ages had she noted
her age or its burden and bounty of expectations.
The future was as flexible as the past,
and, in between, moments like unstrung pearls
strewn across velvet grieved and gladdened her
and always astonished her with their perfection.
There was no nothingness: there was only being.

Slowly she wakes from what had seemed a dream
to realize that this is her final age—
of indeterminate length and quality.
Things are ending, or have ended, or will end.
The pearls are strung with care, it is quite clear.
There is no nothingness—but she can almost,
some days, picture the world without her in it.

WE'D LIKE THEM TO BE DIFFERENT THAN THEY ARE

We'd like them to be different than they are,
those whom we love: more social, quieter;
smarter, less know-it-all, less self-effacing.
More passion would be nice—the kind we like—
with half the current drama. They should be
less nosy, more concerned about our needs.
Sometimes our loved ones make us want to scream
with a small habit that they just can't shake;
it would be wonderful if that were fixed.
They think they're trying hard, but just imagine
what they could become with a bit more effort.

WHAT SORT OF LIGHT

A borrowed brightness blindingly
silvers the sleeping town and field.
What sort of light discovers me,
uncovers me, recovers me,
all while its source remains concealed?

HIS TEETH ON YOUR SYNAPSES

Maybe all of this pain is mercy, mercy, mercy.
That's what you write about your new affliction
(though you have never thought of it as maybe).
The truth, the paradox, the dire connection
between His love and His teeth on your synapses:
for you it's clear that mercy's benediction,
as often as not, will knock us to our knees.
You choose to make of that a genuflection.

PRAYER FOR SISTER CLAIRE

May the Lord bring you a tray of food
each afternoon, draped with a towel
tucked neatly around the edge: a snack,
great care incarnate, manifest love.
May He with intentionality
arrange the dribs and drabs and bites
of all that was best at lunch (having
tenderly set them aside for you)
with a cup of fresh hot coffee. May
you know the same hospitality—
the welcome glad and perpetual,
sustenance with all good things replete—
you both learned at His Mother's feet.

SECOND SUMMER

As Canada burns
all summer and into fall,
what are we to learn?

Breathe slowly. Labor
slowly. Close your eyes. Love but
don't trust your neighbor.

FRAGMENT

The matchstick children, ashen as mud,
curled in the dust and anonymous blood,
gnarled as driftwood, thin as grass:
these rattling children, too, will pass.

They will rise in rapture, grow plump and laugh,
feast with the Father on the fattened calf:
they will dance on their little brown feet one day
The world as we know it is falling away.

THE LAST KIND THING

Soon we will do the last kind thing
and help you out of suffering,
four-legged friend.

But for Aunt Nelda, we will pray
for God to stop her pain today
and make an end.

Hard as it is, we find her pain
an easier thing to entertain
than our own end.

THE TRIOLET IS SUCH A BORE

The triolet is such a bore:
five lines pretending to be eight.
Line one repeats to make line four—
the triolet is such a bore!—
and then line seven. Wait, there's more:
line two will also duplicate.
The triolet is such a bore:
five lines pretending to be eight.

MINUS NINETY-SEVEN

Cold enough to freeze the balls
off a pool table. The temp falls,
"wind-chill factor" kicks in, hard,
dog squats before she hits the yard.
"Keeps Out the Riffraff," our t-shirts say.
(Who dreamed up "wind-chill," anyway?)
Any ass out in all this weather
deserves three toes and skin like leather.
We snowmobile to jobs and bars,
let our taps drip, plug in our cars,
bundle our kids till they can't bend over,
curl up with Jim Beam and Russell Stover.
All of this—and the cold still wins.
We're being punished for our sins
puff the dour preachers stiff with fear.
Well, Armageddon outta here.

ABOUT THE POET

Jane Greer (1953-2025) was a poet ferociously dedicated to her craft. In 1981 she founded *Plains Poetry Journal*, a quarterly literary magazine that was an advance guard of the New Formalism movement. She remained its editor through all its years of publication.

Jane's poems appeared in many periodicals and in three collections: *Bathsheba on the Third Day* (1986), *Love like a Conflagration*, and *The World as We Know It Is Falling Away* (2022).

Born in Iowa, she moved to South Dakota in her last year of high school. She began studies at South Dakota State University and finished her degree at Mary College (now the University of Mary) in Bismarck, North Dakota. She was devoted to the Great Plains and considered herself a regionalist as much as a formalist. Her magazine was named for the

Plains, though its contributors were scattered throughout the world. For *Chronicles* magazine she wrote a monthly column titled "Letter from the Heartland." Late in life, she held court on Twitter (and then X) as NorthDakotaJane.

Her first book, *Bathsheba on the Third Day*, appeared in 1986 to the praise of reviewers. One critic noted the "perfection" of her poems and the "novelty of approaches Greer uses to handle the oldest of themes." "More impressive even than the traditional craft," he went on to say, is "the raw fact" of a particular poem "having been imagined."

In the same years, on a tour of Great Britain, she met the man she would marry: Jim Luptak, who held a master's degree in literature and shared Jane's passion for books.

When she and Jim adopted their son, Robert, Jane made the decision to stop writing. She said that during this time she was not even tempted to produce a poem, and she never even jotted a line. She worked as a civil servant and quietly did good at the margins of her community, among the homeless and in prisons.

Eventually she became a Catholic and then an Oblate, a lay member of the Benedictines, who helped out with small jobs at the local monastery. She survived a serious bout of cancer and began again to write reviews and essays.

Then, just as suddenly as her poetry had stopped, it started anew, after twenty years of silence. In 2019, Jane was sitting in a café in

New Orleans when a poem came to her. By the hotel pool, she sensed another taking shape. Afterward they flowed steadily till the end of her life.

In a 2019 email, she wrote: "It's the poet's job to (1) TRY to see this world as the face and body of a loving God and then (2) TRY to communicate that vision in words. Go big or go home, right?"

To promote her collections she embarked in 2022 on a multi-state tour of readings — in spite of being hobbled by a broken femur. She jokingly called it her "Triumphal March."

Jane's final illness was brief, less than two weeks in which she underwent five surgeries.

This volume, *Nearly a Caress*, brings together her previously uncollected poems, a single fragment, and some poems that were unpublished or unfinished at the time of her death. Her friend and colleague, Robert Bernard Hass, provided editorial guidance in the gathering and arrangement of these last works.

So gently she came out
Almost a whisper of a sound
She mingled with the stillness
And I watched her with feelings profound
I long to see her again
Drink her beauty
A cup as before
Such that I had become drunk
I long for her
Agonize
My love

I love you now
I miss you every hour
When you think of the miles between us
My heart is in want
Your love and beauty
I long to hold you in my arms
The days are long and wasted without you
I miss you so

I have never been with such a beautiful woman
When I look at her
My breath is taken
I cannot drink her in enough
I can't believe she is mine
She is every man's fantasy
I love her so

The wind blows slightly and tells us it is there
The passion that is bred
Only we can know

My beauty brings dawn's day
Her smile warms my life
She bestows happiness
I watch her throughout the day
Her moves
Her empyrean silhouette
Her look
She is my love and inspiration

How does one reflect on life's experiences?
How does one equate love?
Love with the perfect woman
Eyes that drink you in
Her face is like looking at a sunrise
Indescribable beauty
Her body
Love's unquenchable desire
Desire, love I only have for her

When the lamp is shattered
The light in the dust lies dark
When the cloud is scattered
The rainbow's glory is she
Yet when hearts are mingled
Strength of the bond endures all
The sweet emotion conquers all of life's trials
Two, hand in hand, face the storms that rock the ravens on high

I have lived in darkness for so long
Just waiting for the light
And now you have come my way
My days do not seem like nights
I love you

A single rose of love
A single resident devotion
Single wish upon my lips
A single thought of you

A single love
Never to be broken

Into my world of darkness and silence
You brought light and love
When you lit my candle
I began to understand the texture of your love—you are the being
    of my life

The morning dawn's gray
Soft rain pats my face
The clouds gather their cold cloak
But for me, my heart burns with an intense desire of my love
Her beauty an image I desire
Her love breaks the clouds awake
The sun shines in my life as the warmth of her love

My love is the morning light
It pours over me like her exotic body—kissing, probing, yearning
The passion of kisses feeling all the mounds of pleasure, falling into
    ecstasy
And then dark

My love
You are my fresh spring
You wake my senses and make me see life's wonders
You are in my thoughts each day
Allowing me to deal with my confrontations
You are my perfect
As I survey my life
Accomplishments have been many
But now I have found a love
A beauty beyond compare
A woman of exotic features

One whom I love with my heart
Iron Man sits in the cool night
1 see through thc mist her walking being
She approaches
We kiss
I broil her in my passion
My love
My one

My love sleeps in his amiss her dreams
Sunlit beams caress her face
I awake her with kisses sweet
My love for her goes very

She awakens with kisses light
And in her eyes
I see the love she feels
We are one
A bond no one can break

My heart aches as I miss the one I love
My lips long for the feel of your kiss
The feel of your skin
Your gentle touch
The sound of yourself breathing
As you sleep in quiet repose, keep my love
The perfect creation
It is she who moves my life

Spoken words cannot express
How one can feel
Love as that
One cannot be portrayed
The drink of beauty
Its smell
Its feel

Its fire brings life
The heart races at first sight
The night strains ahead
We have experienced true bliss
What love can give

As the days move by
I still am in awe that you are mine
I look at my love
Her golden hair
Her emerald eyes
Her exotic body
Our love rains the love that can be expressed
I, each day, gift to you my love
The joy of your mutual love is what sustains my daily life
Your kiss, your voice
Your beauty
Our passion that is expressed in our bodies' touch
Only you, my beautiful princess
Only you

My beauty lies sleeping
She is so peaceful
So many times have I loved her
Yet I yearn for her love
I think of her always.. . be my life to her and her life
She is my being
My soul
I want her
I want to pleasure her always
I love

There is a certain young lady who manifests the bloom of her beauty
She is teasing
And, yes, so pleasing
Her hair of gold, her lips like spring fruit
Her body
A haven of voluptuous delight
A smile so serene
May life bless her
May nothing in this world distress her
I who behold
And have drunk from the pool
I am in all that all

My morning love
Her beauty is like spring's arrival
Her birthday is cool
Warm
Scents of hyacinth
Daffodils bow to her soft approach
Princess of nature's beauty and love

The morning sky with clouds of pink
Contrasts the beauty of blue
The morning air is brisk but reveals the warm breath of the sun
My love awakes
Her eyes, green, bend the colors of morning
I wait to greet her
My love, my beauty, my princess

The storm clouds gather with a black cloak
They encompass and spend their fury
Protection from the storm comes for beauty
Her petals of white blossoms drenched with rain
Will be dried by the sun's rays
Her prince secures her with his body and kisses

I tell her of my love
While half asleep
In the dark hours
With half words whispered low
I think of her beauty
A year in for her love
I think of her touch
Her talk
I think of our times
When we were one
My love
My beauty
I am hers

Could it be
That once 1 saw you
You were a dream come true?
Could it be I found you
After looking my entire life?
The soft beauty
The gentle touch
The passion that binds us
How could this be?
We want the line separate
Only to know the passion that existed beneath
Yes, a volcano
That has now erupted
I love you so

I know a beauty who, at dusk, begins her sensuous love
The amber light of the moon cloaks her body's silhouette
She is so sensuous
I am aroused by her mystique as she moves through the nightshade
Her love blending with the Farrell flowers of night
My beauty
Whom I love
Whose love I bathe in nightly wonder

My love sleeps in the slumber of peace
I said close
Watching her
Or soft breathing
Her body clings to her covers
Moving gently, stimulating my. ..feelings
I love her so
What I do is for her
She is mobilized my life be if she will be mine
And my life will begin

As the morning sun cracks the new dawn
So am I with my life
With her
My love
My beauty
My one
She is with me as I cross the salo sands
As I cross the meadow
She is there
As we lie among the lilies
We embrace in passion's delight
My love
Life's breath

The beauty is to me
Like the ocean cliffs
She gently perfumes her soft breath as the hyacinth her
Her beautiful face
Her body like a sea
Flowing, drawing me
To her exotic wonders
Listless ecstasy awaits
She is my life

She walks in beauty
Like the night
Cloudless skies and starry climbs A
ll that is best of dark and light
Is in her eyes
How pure, how dear she is to me
How much I yearn for her kiss be, how much her touch electrifies
    me

Her beauty is evermore
My love

Close your eyes
And touch my skin
And feel my
Beating heart
For that is where my love for you will start
I gaze at her in slumber
Posed in peace
I hear her soft breathing
My breath but takes
I kiss your soft lips Drenched in morning dew
I drink from them as a man who never has
I love her as one never ever has

I feel the warm breeze of fall's early wind
I am entering the autumn of my life. My love blossoms with spring's
    beauty
She is her youth
Flowers in her hair critique her majestic face
How could two fall so in love
Bonded by desire and compatibility
There are hand in hand
They will face life's trials
Their bonds never broken

What is love?
An emotion that can be something that moves one through the day
Awaiting the next glance
The next touch, the next kiss
It is what happiness
That is expressed in a body's caress

The morning dawn brings its soft light
Desire is my love's face
She moves to its music
Her skin as but velvet
Her body like a landscape
She awakens
I show her my love
I am hers

I wrote your name in the sky
The wind blew it away
I wrote your name in the sand
The waves washed it away
I wrote your name in my heart
In there it shall forever stay

Your friendship and love
All wonderful things
That you have brought into my life
Or like nothing else I have ever known
My heart is complete with the love that we share
Eyes of passion green and tender people, a world of love awaits
Your essential light and touch
Passions burn brightly
Our bodies engage slightly
Our love invites its magic ecstasies
We as extinguished candles
Our love expressed

Sitting here all alone with nobody to talk to
Only me and my heart
Thinking of you, smiling to myself, drifting away to a world
But nobody else than ourselves
I want that world
Just you and me

My love is but the warm air on a fall day
Her hair cut by its gentle breeze
Her face of white porcelain, without a flaw
I gaze at her
I drink her in
Such beauty is rare to behold
She is my friend, my lover, my all

As I embrace you
It seems that you are the only one who exists
I exist because of you
It is not easy in this world
To lose one's way
But, my love, you have been the light
That has shown my way
You are my life
I love you

Sweet tones of love are remembered
When our lips have met
Our accents of love are not forgotten
The splendor of our hearts echoes
Our desires
Such love is so special
Such love accents are not forgotten

Love can be a mystery
Strange, unexplainable, exotic
Why do people reach its depths of containment?

Why do two drink the desires of its creation?
My love, you don't know
You and I, though, are deep in that pool
Have drunk deeply
I want you all the time

Exquisite beauty has been bestowed on your face
Moonlight shines on you
And the soft wind blows its grace
The gentleness of your touch
Brings pangs of want
The magic of your kiss
Brings nature's movement to a stop
Your beauty, my princess
Ethereal bliss

You are the fire that ignites my own
I am on a journey that knows no end
A love, a passion so deeply felt
Come to me, and let me touch you
Let me feel the wonders that your body steeps
Whirling winds of passion flow
Between our worlds, which are apart
I will travel the mists of time
To hold your mind and heart

I love the way you love me
How your love is always true
I love the way you kiss me
Your touch sets me on fire
I love the way you hold me
Such that we will never be apart
I love the way I need you
Such that you are every part of my life

I love the way you take my breath every time I see your face
You're my perfect love
My princess, my being

I kiss my way through the mounds of pleasure
She moans her beauty the like
I pour myself into her gulf
Extolling my love

My love has dwelt among untrodden ways; she has been through
    life's mires
She has lain by the babbling brook
Yet I who love her so
Impart all I have to give
As she is a princess whom life has blessed
And what I give must impart her beauty's soul

The rain pats gently on my face
I look for the sun's warmth
Tears well in my eyes and mix with drops
I know my love is there
She is patiently waiting
I feel her heart
I yearn for her warmth
The sight of her electrifies me; she is my life

If you only knew
How much my love has grown
Our intimate touch
Has brought us close
I remember the day of our first touch
I remember our first embrace
This will never fade

How can one view such beauty?
The very morning light upon her face
Opens its view as if it were a book
The awe of her features
Grasps me into desire

I kiss
And she responds with deep emotion
We are lost
Both a victim of desire and want

The morning dawn breaks
The strong wind blows
The flow of her hair reflects the beauty of her face
This beauty
One who may hunger
1s silent and directed toward one
Who is that one?
His hair tousled by the wind's frenzy
He lies close
Watching her repose
It is I

The morning rays of light break early
I awake and immediate
Thoughts of my desire
Such beauty creases my mind
Her soft skin, silk hair, and voluptuous lips beckon my yearning
The sound of her laugh, the sound of her talk
Remains in my mind
One torn by yearning and desire
My beauty
My life

There is a certain young lady
Capricious, delicious
And you know very well who I mean
She can thrill with a glance
With her eyes entrance
Her walk stirs a frenzy of glance
She is loving and kind
She is a queen

Falling to the ground
Men at her feet
But alas
This lady is mine

I think of my love while half asleep
In the dark hours
With half words whispered low
As she stirs in her winter sleep
Her eyes awaken, and the world is flowers and morning song
Despite the snow
The falling snow

Every minute passes
I miss you
I miss your smile
I miss your face
I miss your lips
Ours is one that has encompassed us both
The passion of our mutual bond
A relation whose bond cannot be broken
We have become one

The orange light of the morning dawn
Breaks across my sleeping beauty
She appears different
Her face, lips, body show confidence
She has been awoken from her sleep
Her prince had
Kissed her
He will now protect her
He will love and give her life's bounty
Little
For what she gives
Beauty, love
Kisses the entrance
She is his princess

She has skin like rose petals
Her body with lines that meet in geometrical perfection
She is one with whom relaxation comes in her casual conversation
A beauty who has been neglected
By younger suitors
How can this be?
Right now, she is a princess
Her prince has found her
Awakened with a kiss
She is appreciated for all she is
My love
My princess

I arise from dreams of my beauty
In the first sweet sleep of night

The winds are breathing low
The stars shine with bright entrance
A spirit in my feet has led me to your chamber door
She is in her pose of breathless sleep
I gaze in love's grip with yearn and want
I let my love in kisses rain
For my princess is my sweet thought
My dream

As I lie awake
I can see your eyes of passion
Green, longing, wanting
Your sensual touch
Your sensual sight
Love is strong in the morning light
Love is uniting

Her...
One word that means so much to me
A simple reach from her
A stolen glance from her
A message left
And my heart soars
My response to her
When a secret kiss
Means I am hers
Her...
My beauty

My love
Her eyes open with the morning sun
Her lips like coral red
Wanting, urging for my drink
Her breasts like the winter snow
Mound in forms of deep desire
Her perfume entrances

Leaving traces of her beauty's presence
I have but one love
A love who entrances my being
My love

Thy beauty hangs on my love
Like splendor about the moon
Her voice
As silver bells
Soft winds brush her silken hair
And the sun bathes her milken skin
As I behold her, I weep
She is a gift
Created by dewy dawn
And the windless heaven gone

At last, when all the summer shines
That warmed the early hours
Your loving fingers seek for mine
And hold them close at last
I count no more my wasted tears
Which leave no echo with their fall
I mourn no more my lonesome years

There are things that fill my mind
That I just cannot seem to forget
Every way you make me feel
The way we looked when our eyes first met
The way you brush past me
And I catch your scent
Our first kiss
All these things rush to my thoughts
It is you
My beauty
My love

You are a butterfly
You have emerged bright and beautiful
Blazing with color
Pink for our love
Red for our hearts, our passions
Your lips
I look in your eyes
I drink peace and calm
We have become as one
A kiss
An embrace
Passion that only we can know

Eyes of passion
Green and tender
A world of love awaits
Your sensual touch
Your sensual sight

Our love is strong
Our love is uniting
Passion burns
We engage our bodies
We flood our senses

What makes love between two?
1s it nature's soft breeze that entwines them?
Is it caresses that move to passion's peak?
Is it intimate relation of their talks!
Their friendship
A bond not to be broken
My love's beauty
She is my lover and friend
I breathe her in

My love is like the rose red
It springs to morning's dew
Its soft petals burn crimson
Its soft petals burn crimson
Its perfume blows sweet
It is but a symbol of love's fury
The love for my beauty

I feel the cold wind
Brush my face
As I turn to leave
A chill goes through me
The thought of my love and leaving her disturbs me
We have been one
I don't want to leave her
But my duty dictates me
I will remember our love's embrace
I will remember her beauty
Such is the warm fire that sustains me

Into my world of darkness and silence
You have brought the sun's light and the beauty of music
When you lit my candle, I began to see the taste and eroticism of
    your love
You are my love

Understand
The feelings you evoke when your eyes meet mine
You gently breathe, and I close my eyes
And feel your love slowly flow over me
All doubts and troubled fears are put to sleep
My beautiful love

You are my comfort
Whom I run to when I feel alone
My love for you knows no bounds
You are my lover
The one I have wished for
You are my inspiration
Each time I look at your beautiful face
My heart races
Wanting you with all my being
You are my life's wonder
My heart

The morning breeze awakes my love
Her hair tousled gently
Her emerald eyes behold nature about her
She is love
Her beauty blends with nature about her
Her hair with the meadow
Her body with the stream
She is my beauty
My one

The language of true love is forever
That's why love will go away never
Love comes to me in my lover's form
And in my heart
My love is true

The sun rises in the morning sky
I wake and face the day's purple haze
My love is awake
She moves in her way
The beauty, the grace foments my life's tempest
She is mine
I love her

Softly
I whisper my passion
Come to me, my beautiful love
I cherish your gentle tenderness
I yearn for your touch
Your soft breath against my face

I await your embrace
My love knows no bounds
I melt into your rapture

1 love you, too, my beauty
It is true, and I'm devoted solely to you
And you only
You are the best lover I have ever had
And that's the truth

Oh, beauty mine
Where are you roaming?
Your true love waits and is adoring
Trip no further, my pretty sweet
Our journey ends as we as lovers meet
Then come and kiss me, my love's delight
As the night's passion I shall bestow
We as one in ecstasy's delight

You are the ferocious fire
That burns as my desire
With passion
A kiss that never stops
A glance that I always take
To behold such beauty

Our fingers entwine like lace on a twine
Our lips meet, and there is no other taste
My love for you knows no bounds
My hunger is the glance, the look
The feel of your body as I drink the passion of your kiss
The passion as my love flows in you
You are the one
My princess
No other

You came into my world
Where there was darkness
You have brought the rays of light
Where there was silence

You have brought the sweet music of love
You have lit a candle
And I now taste the exotic texture of your love

You are my one and only love
I adore you
I kiss your feet
You are my princess
I escort you to all balls
You are the showpiece of my life
The soft wisp of the morning breath

Awakens her from her nocturnal slumber
Her newborn sprung from ephemeral love
Coddles with soft caresses
Her beauty entwines and offers her infant sempiternal love

The soft breath of morning
Captures her flaxen hair
It wisps the cover of her immaculate beauty
Offering him a soniferous sigh
To behold and inculcate in his mind's want
Thus, she is but a fantasy
The frosty lick of the morning air
Awakens her from her irenic slumber
She as repose
To face her life endeavor
Offering peace and tranquility
To her sempiternal love

In life
He was a most extraordinary man
He was redivivus
But all the more now, his skeuomorphic image
Must be destroyed

The soft breath of spring
1s but the dance of the March daffodil
Swaying to the warm wind
She but as the silhouette and now the peripeteia
Her life transformed
Trading her diamond epergne for the aquamarine
True and deep happiness has now occupied her beauty
She is but redivivus

The winds of March
Breathe their cold breath
Awakening the lips of the princess's slumber
She recruits her minions of nature's mirth
Warm breezes with the daffodils laugh
Spring breathes her warm embrace
All clasp at her gown
To breathe the perfume
Of life's Marian month
Sweet nectar
The privileged
Who the cup
The princess offers her sustenance
Of beauty

Yet the tempest storm
Pushes the advance of her desire
She continues on
Through her daily fare
Never to bow to all who bare her
Her continence glows
As she conquers all who encounter her desire

But is the soft breeze
With nature's fragrance
That breathes her life force

She is but life itself
And her beauty blends with the evergreen ford

The amber sky
Breathes her breath of golden mirth
Her eyes awake to a mirage of rainbow's light
Kissing her
And bestows her beauty for all to behold

As fall breathes her crisp breath
Her metanoia brings her full beauty
She lightly wipes the frosted dew from her wanting lips
His kiss but quenches her wanton desire
Sealing the propinquity

The winds blow their torrent
About the bobbing heads
To the arboreal delight
Ataraxia encompasses her wanton soul
She touches with a soft caress
Her metanoia complete

The sun peeks from the eastern sky
Her soft rays kiss the arboreal scape
Her eyes open to drenched flow
Exuding color of the morning light
Her pulchritude unmatched
She is but desire

The frost of the morning dew
Encompasses her want
The warm breath of passion's fury
Awakens and provides body ablution
The wanton touch
Is but his uxorious love

The vast throws of February's breath
Entrail her frosty mirth
Yet passion is but warmth
That provides the milieu to love's want

Her cool breath
Excites her inner want
She exudes insouciance
As her beauty but is a euphony to all but near her
She but is but exigency
To all who behold her

The coming storm
Spews her redolent and scantling breath
The reticent fear entwines the soul's coming
The prince stands on the fury's bluff
His sword drawn
He stands before his desired love
Protecting with interstice bravery
No fear
Only hypnagogic desire
To protect

The constancy of her touch
Is like the gentle waterfall
Guiding my frangible life's path
The pellucid sound brought from her instrument
Are but nature's sound of the opening dawn
The habile skill of a mother's love
Her intent hand guiding my life's direction and passion

Is but part of her redolent nature
The sound of her trumpet
And her life
Will remain imperishable
Unforgotten
Efflorescent

As April breathes her lilac perfume
The hushed sounds of the newborn's mirth
Divaricate across the green pelt of nature's fugacious path
She, the mother, presses softly
Across the infant's cheek
Lovingly gloating into his eyes
She reflects on the miracle
Hypnagogic to her surroundings
Her newfound beauty
Unsurpassed

As the storm gathers its coming fury
So will he stand
Cutting its nebula with a sharp cavalcade
It will not blight his continent being
He will overcome
And walk into the sun
Warm, healed
But the warm breeze
A kiss from the rustling leaves
Softly brushes her hair
Her beauty unfolded, surrounded by the susurrus of her life's
    want
I, the lover, absorb her capricious moods
I am but her prisoner
Lost in blithesome ecstasy

The August breeze offers her flowered breath
It rustles the leaves
Offering their sweet music

She lies on the green velvet of repose
Her face tilted
Observed by soft moonlight
His desire is but wanton in the viewing distance
Observing her sensuous moves
Bathing in her transpicuous cover

And the light
That filters on her silken skin
Reflects the silhouette of nature's want
Cascades of fragrant flow
Entwine with wanton touch
Her lips breviloquent as to sink
To ecstasy

But as the rain will spread her dew
So will love's ember
Carry her warmth through distances of time
Sweet thoughts of embrace

But what is the fragrance of the lilac
Rushing sweet dreams of love's entrance
Moving as the stream to wanton desire
A man
Whose love creates his woven image
Nurtures his life's expectations
He, the father, creates the boy who becomes the man
And such the ignomy
Never can such be put asunder
Never can more love
Bond the soul

But what is birth in the suckle of the warm July?
Parents in deep love
Create the beauty's image
She walks in grace

Silence
Bringing joy to all
She touches
She is but the summer warmth
Caressing all in her continence
My wife
My love

But to battle's call
We who enlist it daily
Have been struck
Left with our internal thoughts, to which no one can relate
But within the strangled agony
We push on
Slowly the warm breeze will restore the pall of health
Wash the gloom of countless days
In spite of all
We shall attain the immortal drink

But as the horizon settles
The smoke of battle remains
Its acrid reminder of the day's fight
Never an inch given
Day to day, the anarchy is slowly broken
The hero arises

For my friend, the hero and the brave
The soft caress of the midnight
Brushes her face
The moon silhouettes the beauty
As she rises from her slumber
Exotic as she moves
She is but the day's continence
Life's day and joy
Her breath as the sweet spring lilac
Drowned in ecstasy of her persistent beauty

But who as the autumn brings its leaves of gold
Must face winter's breath?
Great phantoms of frigid wrath
Freezing the countenance of life's caress
But the breath of spring's warm foray warms the continence of
    life's
Transience

But what is beauty?
It is a fleeting moment of the eyes' candescence
A joy forever
With increasing loveliness
But still will keep
A bough of night's pleasure And sweet sleep
Entwined as two
As melted snow

She rises from her night's slumber
As the sun dries
The morning dew
From her sapphire eyes
Her beauty
As is nature's mirth
Blended with wanted radiance
I watch... I wonder... I dream
My life
But for a father's love
His intent hand
Guiding my thought's passion
Nurtures the education of life
And I succeed as he was my guide
My representative of him
Passion
Love of life as I how to his ever presence

The morning sprinkles its rays
The dew moist from night's respite
Glistens a blinding color from her face
She is but the beauty of nature's fold
Contrast to the world's darkness

But as the rain will spread her dew
So much will love's ember
Carry her warmth through distances of time
Sweet thoughts of embrace

About the Author

Harry John Visser was born on September 22, 1952, in the small rural town of Huntsburg, Ohio. He attended Cardinal High School in Middlefield, Ohio, and graduated in 1970. He then attended Hiram College and graduated magna cum laude with a BA in chemistry. From there, he received his doctorate in podiatric medicine from the Kent State School of Podiatric Medicine in 1978.

Dr. Visser performed his residency in foot and ankle reconstructive surgery from 1978 to 1981 in St. Louis, Missouri. He became a residency director in 1984 and ran the program until 2015 at Mineral Area Regional Medical Center in Farmington, Missouri. He then became director of the SSM DePaul Foot and Ankle Residency Program in 2012 in St. Louis, Missouri. All told, he has trained nine-ty-nine residents and is still serving as director.

Dr. Visser was president of the Missouri Podiatric Medical Association from 1985 to 1988. He was appointed to the State Board of Podiatric Medicine by three governors and served as president on numerous occasions.

Dr. Visser was appointed to the Distinguished Alumni Hall of Fame at Cardinal High School in 2015. He was inducted as a fellow in the Garfield Society at Hiram College in 2017. He was also inducted as the Kent State School of Podiatric Medicine Hall of Fame in 2015.

Dr. Visser is a national and international lecturer, having given presentations in nine different countries. He has published over seventy scientific publications and currently is to have his own book published in 2022.